# SYRIA

# MAJOR WORLD NATIONS
# SYRIA

Martin Mulloy

## CHELSEA HOUSE PUBLISHERS
### Philadelphia

**Chelsea House Publishers**

Copyright © 1999 by Chelsea House Publishers,
a division of Main Line Book Co.
All rights reserved.
Printed in Hong Kong

First Printing.

1 3 5 7 9 8 6 4 2

Library of Congress Cataloging-in-Publication Data

Mulloy, Martin.
Syria / Martin Mulloy.
p. cm. — (Major world nations)
Includes index.
Summary: Explores the people, history, culture, land, climate, and
economy of Syria, a battleground of empires and a country still in
the early stages of independence
ISBN 0-7910-4983-3(hc)
1. Syria—Juvenile literature. [1. Syria.] I. Title.
II. Series.
DS93.M85 1998
956.91—dc21    98-4307
CIP
AC

ACKNOWLEDGEMENTS

The author and publishers are grateful to the following organizations and individuals for
permission to reproduce copyright illustrations in this book:
J. Allan Cash Photolibrary; Hutchison Photo Library; IPA/TRIP; Jamie Kidston/
TRIP;The Mansell Collection Ltd; Frank Spooner Pictures.

# CONTENTS

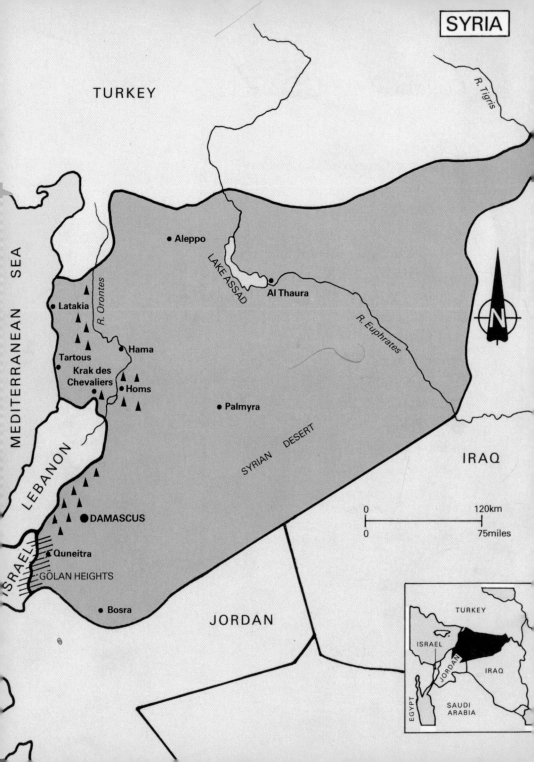

# FACTS AT A GLANCE

## Land and People

| | |
|---|---|
| **Official Name** | Syrian Arab Republic |
| **Location** | Middle East; bordered in the southwest by Lebanon, in the south by Jordan, in the east by Iraq and in the north by Turkey |
| **Area** | 71,430 square miles (185,000 square kilometers) |
| **Climate** | Hot and dry summers; mild and wet winters |
| **Capital** | Damascus |
| **Other Cities** | Aleppo, Homs, Lattakia, Hamah |
| **Population** | 17 million |
| **Population Density** | 209 persons per square mile (81 persons per square kilometer) |
| **Major Rivers** | Euphrates, Tigris |
| **Major Lakes** | Lake al-Assad |
| **Mountains** | Jebel an-Nusariyah, Anti-Lebanon |
| **Official Language** | Arabic |

| | |
|---|---|
| **Other Languages** | Kurdish, Armenian, Turkish, English, French |
| **Religions** | Islam, Greek Orthodox, Roman Catholic, Protestant |
| **Literacy Rate** | 71 percent |
| **Average Life Expectancy** | 68.4 years for males; 71.3 years for females |

## Economy

| | |
|---|---|
| **Natural Resources** | Petroleum, natural gas, iron ore |
| **Agricultural Products** | Cotton, tobacco, various fruits, wheat, barley and tomatoes |
| **Industries** | Mining, fishing, manufacturing, tourism |
| **Major Imports** | Machinery, iron, steel, chemicals, textiles |
| **Major Exports** | Petroleum, vegetables, cotton, textiles |
| **Currency** | Syrian pound (lira) |

## Government

| | |
|---|---|
| **Form of Government** | Unitary multiparty with one legislative house |
| **Government Bodies** | People's Council |
| **Formal Head of State** | President |

# HISTORY AT A GLANCE

**2000 B.C.** A Semitic people, the Phoenicians, inhabit the coastal regions of Syria and Lebanon.

**500 B.C.** Damascus becomes famous for its steel-making, particularly as used in swords and other weapons.

**323 B.C.** Alexander the Great dies and the Middle Eastern part of his empire is ruled by the descendants of his general, Seleucis. Syria is the center of Seleucid power.

**64 B.C.** Syria becomes a Roman province after being conquered by the Roman general Pompey. Roman Syria includes modern Lebanon and Israel.

**661 A.D.** Syria becomes the center of the Muslim world when the Umayyad Dynasty makes its headquarters at Damascus.

**1086** The Seljuk Turks replace the Arab rulers of Iraq and Syria.

**1099** Crusaders from Europe capture Jerusalem from the Muslims. A Crusader kingdom occupies coastal Lebanon, Syria and Palestine for two centuries.

9

| | |
|---|---|
| **1173** | The Kurdish Muslim leader Saladin occupies Damascus as part of his attempt to unify Islam after several years of civil war. He is buried in Damascus in a magnificent mausoleum after his death (1193). |
| **1516** | The Ottoman Turks occupy Damascus as they march on the Egyptian capital of the Mameluke empire. Syria will remain part of the Ottoman Empire until the end of World War I. |
| **1919** | At the end of World War I, French troops occupy Syria. |
| **1920** | Fighting breaks out between the French and local Syrians. |
| **1925-1927** | The Druze people launch a revolt against French rule from the mountains of southeastern Lebanon. Peace returns after two years of fighting which included serious clashes in Damascus. |
| **1942** | The Baathist movement is founded in Syria. |
| **1946** | Independence is achieved as the French withdraw. |
| **1948** | Syria joins in the Arab attack on the new state of Israel, without success. |
| **1949** | Defeat by the Israelis and internal dissensions lead to eleven years of instability, including thirteen coups and coup attempts. |
| **1954** | Baathists in the military come to power for the first time. |
| **1958** | Syria unites with Egypt to form the United Arab Republic. |
| **1967** | After a brief round of fighting, Syria loses the |

Golan Heights area to Israel during the Six-Day War.

**1971** Defense Minister Hafez Al-Assad seizes power after a long period of unrest. Although his rule is often autocratic, Syria experiences a long period of prosperity and stability.

**1973** Syria joins with Egypt in its attempt to regain the Sinai from Israel.

**1976** Syria intervenes in Lebanon's civil war.

**1980s** Syria supports Iran in the Iran-Iraq conflict that drags on through most of the decade.

**1991** Syria joins the coalition against Iraq during the Persian Gulf crisis.

**1990s** Syrian relations with most Western countries steadily improve. Negotiations with Israel continue, but remain deadlocked over the issue of Israeli withdrawal from the Golan Heights.

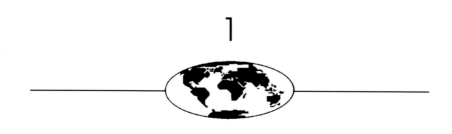

# Syria—the Crossroads of History

Syria is a country of great antiquity. The landscape is littered with the ruins and remains of some of the world's earliest civilizations. To visit Syria is to visit a land where the modern and the extremely ancient stand side by side. The name "Syria" has existed from the earliest times: the actual land that it describes has often changed shape and size. Sometimes it included parts of what are now Lebanon, Israel, Iraq and Turkey.

For thousands of years Syria has been the battleground of empires. The country was a rich prize—blessed with fertile lands, the crossroads of great trade routes, the marketplace of East and West, the site of holy places and the birthplace of sophisticated civilizations. Many different peoples and empires have invaded, occupied and colonized Syria. Most of them left their mark, whether in the wonderful ruins which dot the landscape or in other, more subtle ways: in traditions of food, clothing, handicrafts and architecture. Despite all this, for over a thousand years the essential character of the Syrian people has remained the same—Arab and Muslim. Today the Syrian Arab Republic, as it is officially called, is an independent state with recognized borders and is a member of the United Nations. It is surprising to realize that this country, whose history goes back to the dawn of time, has only been independent since 1946.

The earliest civilizations developed here. Syria was part of the area known as the "Fertile Crescent," an arc of land covering parts of Turkey, Syria and Iraq. The land was arable, watered by rainfall and by great rivers, and it provided a good environment for people to settle. The people who settled here thousands of years ago had previously been nomadic (travelling with their herds in search of grazing and water). In the course of time, however, they developed complex civilizations along the green banks of the Euphrates and Tigris rivers. These civilizations flourished long before the birth of Christ—some existed as far back as 5000 B.C. It was here that the first known alphabet was invented, and here that the first writing and legal systems developed. In many ways, the ancient lands in and around Syria were the cradle of civilization. Damascus itself, the capital of Syria, is reckoned to be the world's oldest continuously inhabited city.

Syria is a living museum of its own history. To travel around Syria is to see the remains of ages gone by: distant civilizations, the aftermath of battles, the left-overs of empires. From the recently excavated ancient cities near the Euphrates to the fabulous ruins of Palmyra (the desert city of Queen Zenobia),

14

**Bedouin with their sheep at a watering-hole in the Syrian desert. The first people to settle in the area of present-day Syria thousands of years ago were nomads such as these, who had travelled vast distances with their herds in search of water and grazing.**

from the Roman amphitheaters and columns at Bosra to the huge castles and citadels of Saladin and the Christian Crusaders, from early Christian churches to grand mosques—all Syria is rich with the sights and monuments of its own history.

Many great figures from world history have been part of Syrian history: Nebuchadnezzar, the King of ancient Babylon; Cyrus the Great, King of Persia; Alexander the Great; Pompey, Julius Caesar and Mark Antony; Saint Paul; the Prophet Muhammad, founder of Islam; Saladin, the Arab leader during the Crusades; Richard the Lionheart, King of England and Crusader; Tamerlane, the leader of the Mongols; and, in the twentieth century, T. E. Lawrence (Lawrence of Arabia). The list of peoples who have invaded or occupied Syria is equally dramatic: Egyptians, Babylonians, Persians, Greeks, Romans, Arabs, European Crusaders, Mongols from Central Asia, Turks, French and British.

Damascus and Syria played a large part in the early history of Christianity. There is still a thriving Christian community as well as many ruined churches and monuments dating back to Biblical times. Saint Paul "saw the light" on the road to Damascus and stopped his persecution of the Christians to become one himself. Both Damascus and Syria are mentioned often in the Bible. Indeed, in the hill village of Maalula, northwest of Damascus, the people speak Aramaic, the actual language spoken at the time of Jesus.

It was after the birth of the Islamic religion in the seventh century A.D., however, that Damascus achieved its greatest glory. The city became the first capital of an Islamic empire that spanned most of the known world. It was an age of great learning and of magnificent architecture. The beautiful mosque in Damascus was built at this time. This glorious past as the heart of the Islamic empire is still part of the Syrian heritage. To this day, Syria is essentially an Arab and a Muslim country.

Although part of the Fertile Crescent, today's Syria is also two-thirds desert. The Syrian desert overlaps frontiers and goes deep into the heart of the Arabian peninsula. It is home to the Bedouin, the nomadic tribesmen who have wandered these parched wastes since the beginning of recorded history. Syria has always been a mixture of city-dweller, peasant and nomad. The

**A young Bedouin girl.**

proportions have changed today, with most people living in towns and cities, but much of what is essentially Syrian remains.

Side by side with ancient Syria is modern Syria—a country still in the early stages of independence, still developing, still progressing. New highways and railway tracks cut through the old battlefields. Giant new hydroelectric dams control the flow of the mighty Euphrates—the river whose waters helped give birth to early civilizations. New tower-blocks of offices and apartments spring up in Damascus and other cities, overshadowing buildings a thousand years old or more. New wars are fought on the sites of old. Syria has been at war with Israel several times since independence and also became deeply engaged in the Lebanese

17

conflict. The history of the country and the region is still a troubled history—and yet, in the midst of all this, modern Syria remains a fast-developing and changing nation.

Ancient Syria, Greek Syria, Roman Syria, Christian Syria, Islamic Syria, the Syria of the Crusaders, Mongol Syria, Turkish Syria, French Syria—there are many Syrias and they belong to different eras and centuries and involve various races, religions and empires. Like a complicated piece of historical arithmetic, the modern Syria of today is their sum total.

# 2

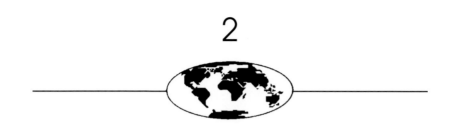

# The Land

Syria lies at the eastern end of the Mediterranean Sea. It shares borders with Turkey to the north, Iraq to the east and Jordan to the south. In the southwest, it borders on Israel and Lebanon. It also has about 100 miles (160 kilometers) of coastline on the eastern shore of the Mediterranean. Syria has an area of approximately 70,000 square miles (185,000 kilometers). In a geographical sense, as well as a historical sense, Syria forms a link between the continents of Asia, Africa and Europe.

The population of the country is around seventeen million. The majority of people used to live in the countryside, although nowadays the cities of Syria are growing rapidly and urban life is becoming more and more common. The people who inhabit Syria come from many different racial backgrounds. The majority, however, are Arab in origin.

The land is made up of several distinct natural regions. These include coastal plains, mountain chains, huge tracts of desert,

19

high fertile plains, river valleys and grassy uplands. In ancient times, parts of Syria belonged to the "Fertile Crescent"—an arc of green and rich land which stretched from Turkey, down the river valleys of Syria and Iraq to the Arabian Gulf. This vast area of land was nourished by rainfall in the northern parts and irrigated by the waters of the two great rivers in the south, the Euphrates and Tigris. For thousands of years the land has been farmed. In ancient times it was called the "breadbasket of civilization." To this day, some of the same land in Syria is intensively cultivated.

On the eastern shore of the Mediterranean, in the western part of Syria, is the Plain of Lattakia. The plain covers a large area and is home to a strong agricultural community. Orange and lemon groves, orchards and vegetable fields are everywhere. The land is green and fertile. Other crops include dates, grapes, olives, figs and tobacco. This narrow coastal plain is hemmed in by a mountain chain running from north to south. These mountains help to trap the rain-bearing clouds which water the Plain of Lattakia. On the slopes of the mountains, terraces have been carved out so as to cultivate as much land as possible. It is no accident that a large part of the Syrian population lives near the coast: the climate is good and temperate and the land is fertile.

Not all of the coastal plain is farmland. To the north of the port city of Lattakia, the coastline is dramatic and rugged with rocky cliffs. Some of this coastline is connected to the mountain range which runs from north to south, parallel to the Plain of Lattakia. The range is called Jebel Ansariya. The highest peak, at the northern end of the range, is Nabi Yunis which is over 15,000 feet (1,500 meters) high. The source of the Orontes River is located in the mountains. It flows northward towards the Turkish border. The valley of the Orontes was once marshlands but now it has been transformed. Drainage and new irrigation schemes have helped to turn the area into one of the market gardens of Syria.

Another major mountain range runs along the border between Syria and Lebanon. The range is known as the Anti-Lebanon. The highest peak in all Syria is found here. It is Mount Hermon, mentioned in the Bible, and it reaches a height of over 9,000 feet

(2,750 meters). The Jebel Druze, another mountain range, is located in the southeast. This mountain area forms the home of one of Syria's minority peoples–the Druzes. The rugged landscape has been a defence for the Druze people throughout history and has long given them protection and helped them to survive.

Syria, then, has several key mountain areas; they play a varied part in the making of the country. They act as natural barriers for rain-clouds, thus making nearby plains fertile, and they are an important source of rivers and streams. At the same time they have provided refuge in troubled times for certain small sections of the population.

A great deal of central Syria is high grassy plateaux. These areas of grassland are called steppes. The steppes are reminiscent

**A remote village in the Jebel Ansariya mountains.**

of parts of Europe and Russia. These areas have very few trees and little rain falls here during the year. Because of the altitude, the climate is generally cold and windy. In winter, snow may cover much of the land. Although the steppes are not good for cultivation, they are ideal for grazing flocks of sheep and goats. This windswept, almost tree-less, landscape where shepherds tend sheep, goats and camels can seem like a scene from the Bible.

It is here, and in the desert into which the grassy steppes merge, that the nomadic Bedouin live. The Bedouin live in tents, and move constantly with their flocks in search of grazing and water. The steppes and the desert cover the majority of Syria. They are fit for neither cultivation nor settlement. Most of the grassy steppes are in the northern half of Syria and on average they are over 2,000 feet (600 meters) above sea level. To the south and east, the steppes gradually disappear into the seemingly endless ocean of sand which forms the Syrian desert.

The desert is huge, extends far into Iraq and Jordan and continues deep into Saudi Arabia in the south. Although there are borders between the countries, the desert itself knows no frontiers. Like an ocean, it moves constantly, changing shape with the wind. It can be very beautiful but it can also be inhospitable. Temperatures are extremely high and only a few animals survive here—snakes, scorpions, lizards and jackals. The only people to "inhabit" the desert are the Bedouin. Round about their tents are their flocks and—perhaps their only concession to the modern world—a pick-up truck or jeep. The

**A shepherd and his flock in the steppes of central Syria.**

Bedouin are like the desert they inhabit—ever-moving and recognizing no frontier. They form only a small part of the Syrian population.

Within the steppes and the desert there are oases. Sometimes these are nourished by rivers and sometimes by underground springs and wells. They are like fertile islands in a barren ocean. One of the other key fertile zones is around the capital, Damascus. The oasis here is fed by the Barada River. It is in the north of the country, however, that two of Syria's most important geographical features are found.

Two of the most mighty and famous rivers in the world flow through the Syrian landscape—the Euphrates and the Tigris. These rivers played a huge part in the history not only of the region but

24

of eastern and western civilization. The ancient name of Iraq and northeast Syria was Mesopotamia. This was a Greek word meaning "between two rivers." The rivers made the land fertile and brought prosperity which helped to create and enrich ancient civilizations such as Babylon. Today they also play a vital part in the development of Syria.

The Euphrates, in particular, is now the main source of electrical power in Syria. The huge Euphrates Dam is reckoned to be one of the biggest in the world. The river itself flows from its source in Turkey through Syria and into Iraq. The Tigris also flows through northeast Syria on a roughly parallel course with the Euphrates until the two rivers join in Iraq, and flow into the waters of the Arabian Gulf.

The areas along the riverbanks are not densely populated. There are, however, many small villages and farming

**The Euphrates Dam, reckoned to be one of the biggest in the world.**

communities dotted along the course of the rivers. New irrigation schemes will increase the fertile fields and there are plans to repopulate the area as its agricultural potential is developed. As in the Plain of Lattakia, common crops in this area are wheat, millet, barley, maize and cotton.

The climate of Syria is varied. The most important factor is rainfall. Wherever rain falls in sufficient quantities, the land is green and able to support crops and people. Where there is little or no rain, only the nomadic Bedouin and their flocks will survive. The Plain of Lattakia has a Mediterranean climate with mild winters, good rainfall and summers cooled by sea breezes. Slightly inland, in the mountains and valleys, the rainfall is heavier; and the streams which pour down from the mountains help to make the plains below fertile. Further inland, the rainfall is very slight. The high steppes get only enough rain to produce grass, and the desert receives hardly any rain at all.

One surprise, however, is that snow regularly falls in the mountain zones. The contrast in landscape and climate can be so marked in Syria that it is possible to stand in the hot desert and view snow-capped mountains in the distance.

Throughout the country there is also a wide variety of plants and animals. Some of the mountain valleys have forests. Oak, pine, cedar and cypress trees are common. In the steppes the small terebinth tree grows. This tree is the source of turpentine. Indeed, the English word turpentine is derived from the name of the tree. There are many different species of wildlife. Deer, gazelles, wildcats and foxes can be found in the mountains. Birds, too, are varied.

Hawks, kites, pelicans, flamingos and game birds are all common. In the desert, there are even ostriches.

The key mineral and natural resources of Syria are oil, phosphates, salt, gypsum and asphalt. Oil was discovered only recently, in the 1950s, and is now a major part of the economy.

Syria, therefore, possesses a wide variety of landscape and climate: fertile plains and snow-capped mountains, windy uplands and vast, scorching deserts, gentle green oases and majestic rivers. These different aspects of the landscape, especially the rivers and mountains, have played an important part in the history of the country and its people.

# 3

# The People

The people of Syria are mostly Arab. The vast majority, over eighty-five percent, are Muslims who believe in the religion of Islam. At the same time the Syrian population is a complex mix of other races and religions. Over thousands of years, Syria has been invaded and occupied by many other peoples, and today's population reveals many traces of Syria's checkered history. There is a significant percentage of non-Arab groups. These are mainly Kurds, Armenians, Circassians and Turks. Similarly, there are also people of other religions: unorthodox Muslims such as the Druzes, Alawites and Ismailis, as well as a wide variety of Christian groups.

While most of the people are Mediterranean and Arab in appearance with dark hair, eyes and complexions, there are also blond and red-haired Syrians, as well as black-skinned ones. The main language is Arabic but many people, especially in the cities, also speak some French. Other languages and dialects are also used, such as Aramaic (the ancient language which was spoken at the time of Christ), Armenian and Kurdish.

**A Syrian man in traditional Arab dress.**

The Arabs, who form the majority of Syria's seventeen million or so inhabitants, can trace their ancestry back to the period of Arab conquest following the birth of Islam. Islam was founded by the Prophet Muhammad in the seventh century A.D. Muhammad was a citizen of Mecca (in present-day Saudi Arabia) who believed he was a prophet, or messenger of God. He claimed that God spoke to him and told him to preach the true word of God. The message which Muhammad relayed to the citizens of Mecca warned them to stop worshipping false pagan gods and idols and to turn to the one, true God. Gradually the new religion attracted converts. From its small beginnings Islam grew rapidly and, in the years after Muhammad's death, the new message of God was carried by

29

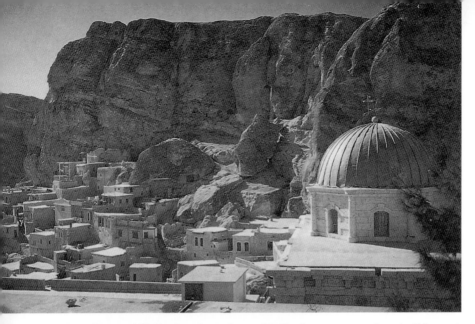

**The village of Malloula where Aramaic, the language spoken in this part of the world at the time of Christ, is still spoken.**

victorious Arab armies to Morocco and Spain in the west and as far as India in the east. Syria became a central part of the new Islamic empire. With Islam came the Arabic language.

And yet there were Arabs in Syria before Islam. It is thought that the word "Arab" and the word "Hebrew" come from a similar language root and mean "wanderer." Certainly, the nomadic Bedouin have been part of Syrian culture for thousands of years. Islam and the Arabic language, however, did much to unite the people of the region.

In the thousands of years before the seventh century A.D., Syria had been invaded and occupied by Babylonians, Persians, Greeks, Romans and others. This led to a complex mixture of

30

races: the make-up of the population was ever-changing. It was only after the triumph of Islam that the people who were living in the region could be said to share the same racial and religious background.

In addition to the overwhelming majority of Muslims following the orthodox Islam practiced most commonly elsewhere in the Arab world, there are other Muslim sects—the Alawites, Druzes and Ismailis. They are found in various parts of the country. The Alawites, for instance, are numerous around the Mediterranean port of Lattakia, while the Druzes live mostly in the mountain district of Jebel Druze. Although the religious practices of these groups are very different from those of the orthodox Muslims in

**A Druze village in the mountain district of Jebel Druze.**

the rest of Syria, they are generally accepted as part of the overall Muslim community.

Another significant part of the population, just over ten percent, are Christian. The largest groups belong to the Greek Orthodox, Armenian Orthodox and Syrian Orthodox churches. Other Christian groups include Catholics and Protestants, and there are also some Jews. Compared to some other Middle Eastern countries, Syria can boast a wide variety of religious beliefs.

Today in Syria there are Armenians from Turkey, people of Greek descent, and in the northeast (near the Iraqi and Turkish borders), the Kurds. The Armenians are Christians who fled Turkey to avoid oppression and persecution early this century. Over 100,000 settled in the region around Aleppo. The Kurds are Muslims. They are an ancient people and have always inhabited the region where Syria, Iraq and Turkey come together. Their total number is several million but only about 100,000 live in Syria. They are a mountain people with their own distinct language and culture. Another racial group in Syria is the Circassians. They trace their ancestry back to Russia from where they fled to avoid persecution. They are also Muslims. Very often they are fair-haired and fair-skinned and European in appearance.

Despite being predominantly Arab, Syria is also a rich ethnic mix compared to many other Middle Eastern countries.

The greatest change in twentieth-century Syria has been the gradual drift from the villages and the country to the cities.

**A small Syrian village.**

Nowadays, just over half the population lives in cities and large towns. Previously the majority were peasants, working the land and fields and living in small villages. As Syrian society and industry have developed, however, more and more people have come to the cities; to Damascus, Aleppo, Homs, Hama, Lattakia, Tartous and others. This does not necessarily mean that the rural areas are dying. On the contrary, new agricultural developments and agriculturally-related industries are being established in rural and distant provinces to slow down the drift of people from the villages to the towns, and to provide new work for the country people.

The population itself is growing fast. According to a World Bank survey, Syria has one of the highest population growth rates in the world. This is due to many factors, most notably the increase in health care and life expectancy.

Another great change in recent years has been the provision of compulsory education for children. Syria is now developing an extensive education system, and the number of primary and secondary schools has grown dramatically. Like many developing countries, Syria realizes that its greatest asset is its own people. Technical colleges, industrial training centers and universities have been established throughout the country. One encouraging factor is the high percentage of female students. Women make up one third of the 60,000-plus students at Damascus University. Throughout Syrian society, women have greater opportunities than most of their counterparts elsewhere in the Arab world.

The dramatic growth in education has been a necessary response to the problems which Syria faced in the early days of independence. Illiteracy (the inability to read or write) was high. This has now been reduced considerably. Similarly, there were problems in starting new industrial projects because of a shortage of well-trained and qualified manpower. Progress in education in the last few decades has been the real foundation of Syrian development.

Many of these changes in the Syrian way of life, the drift from country to city, the better health and education systems and the modernizing of the country, are comparatively recent. Some of them have happened in the space of a single generation. Today, the Syrian way of life encompasses extremes: from the sophisticated citizens of Damascus, Aleppo and Lattakia to the peasants, shepherds and Bedouin all living lives relatively unchanged for centuries.

With the break-up of the older pattern of life in Syria there have come other changes. Most city-dwellers now live in modern high-rise apartment blocks whereas previously they lived in a variety of dwellings. In the west, near the forested valleys, wooden houses were common. In northern Syria, mud-brick homes, sometimes conical in shape like beehives, were more typical because of the lack of wood. (The mud bricks also meant that the houses were cool in hot summers.) The shepherds and Bedouin still live in their long, black tents.

All these different styles of living can still be seen but modern Syria is now changing rapidly. In some parts of Damascus, apart from the language of the street signs, a stranger could be forgiven for thinking he was in a European city. Much of the new building style in the cities is international and the office blocks, hotels, banks and apartment blocks look like those found elsewhere in all parts of the world. Yet the same stranger could turn a corner and find a scene which is ageless: simple shepherds and Bedouin praying in the cool shade of a thousand-year-old mosque, or merchants haggling over the cost of spices in a market that dates from Biblical times.

Syria is a mixture of times and ages as well as races and religions. It has always been a melting-pot of peoples. The diversity of races, religions and languages is part of the richness of Syria.

# 4

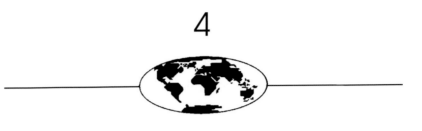

# Syria in Ancient Times

Travelling through Syria today, it is possible to see the ruins and remains of many civilizations of the distant past. The history of Syria is visible everywhere; the surprising thing is the astonishing richness, variety and great age of many of the ruins. In the north of the country there are archaeological sites dating back to beyond 2500 B.C. The latest evidence from these sites suggests that the civilization there was as sophisticated and complex as the Egypt of the Pharaohs.

In the thousands of years since then, there have been many other civilizations in Syria. At various times, Egyptians, Babylonians, Persians, Greeks, Romans, Arabs, Europeans and Turks have all been involved in Syria. Some fought battles there for control of trade routes or holy places, some possessed it as part of a wider empire, some were there only briefly and others for over a thousand years.

Ancient cities are now slowly being unearthed around the Euphrates River in the north. Ruined palaces, Roman

**Palmyra, lying isolated in the middle of the desert, is one of the most completely preserved ancient cities in the world.**

amphitheaters, the desert city of Palmyra, thousand-year-old mosques, Christian monasteries, gigantic Crusader castles—all these are part of Syria's heritage.

In ancient times, the land known as Syria covered a greater area of land than the present-day Syrian Arab Republic. The Syria of antiquity, or "Greater Syria" as it is sometimes known, also covered much of the land of neighboring countries. The changing size of the land was determined by various factors—in particular by wars and the power and influence of certain civilizations. The geographical area of Greater Syria has been one of the world's great battlegrounds throughout history. Its

37

importance as a prize can be traced to two main reasons—its location in the rich, green heartland of the Fertile Crescent and at the crossroads of the great trade routes of the ancient world.

Syria was always a link between Asia, Africa and Europe. It was the natural destination and trading-point on the key trade routes: the Spice Route and the Silk Route.

The Spice Route originated in the far south of Arabia, in Yemen. Spices such as frankincense and myrrh came from this region. Frankincense was used in countless religious rituals throughout most ancient civilizations; it was also used for cosmetic reasons and was the basis of most perfumes. This spice was one of the most valued commodities of the ancient world. Huge camel caravans carried it through the great Arabian deserts. Damascus and Aleppo were the main trading and distribution points.

Similarly, silk from China and the East came to Syria. Damascus itself was famous for the production of a rich silk brocade known as damask. In cities like Aleppo, vast markets sprang up, servicing an international trade. People from all the corners of the known world lived and traded there. Both Damascus and Aleppo grew rich and powerful from this trade. It was a lucrative business and many battles were fought to gain control of the routes.

As a part of the Fertile Crescent, Greater Syria was richly endowed with food. The fact that the land was green and cultivatable meant that conditions were ideal for people to settle there. These early settled communities provided the basis for the development of more advanced civilizations. It is no exaggeration to say that this area was the most important site in the early history of mankind.

Throughout this area, there developed the first agriculture, the first major cities, the first alphabets and written languages and the first empires. As civilizations developed and grew, they fought for control of the fertile lands.

In the beginning, the various peoples who migrated towards the riverbanks of the Euphrates and the Tigris were originally nomadic tribes—Sumerians, Babylonians, Canaanites, Arameans, Hebrews and Nabataeans. Collectively these people are now known by the term Semites; this means they were descended from Shem, the son of Noah. Today we describe the people of the Middle East as Semitic. In the fertile lands these tribes settled and ceased wandering. In the thousands of years that followed, others did the same. Syria became a melting-pot: Egyptians, Persians, Greeks, Romans, Mongols and Turks all became intermixed.

The first great Syrian city rose in the northeast on the banks of the Euphrates. It is known as the Mari civilization and it dates back to about 2500 B.C. It has only recently been discovered and excavated. The sophistication and size of this city-state can only be guessed at but the King's palace had over three hundred rooms. Over twenty thousand clay tablets were also dug up, bearing the language of the people. The writing was known as cuneiform. It was difficult to master and contained hundreds upon hundreds of signs meaning different things. It was more of a sign code, like Egyptian hieroglyphs, than a written language.

The excavated city also possessed temples, statues, ceramic baths with a running water system, libraries and banks. While most of the people in Europe were living in primitive mud huts, there were cities in Syria which boasted a quarter of a million inhabitants.

Another city-civilization in Syria was called Ugarit. It was located on the coast, near present-day Lattakia. The very first, simple and practical alphabet was developed here. Tablets containing the alphabet have been dug up. Today, these original tablets can be seen in the National Museum in Damascus. The alphabet was written with a pen made from a reed and contained thirty letters or signs to represent the sound of consonants. Many other alphabets are thought to have sprung from the Ugarit alphabet by adapting the shapes of the letters.

The ancient empires rose and fell and were sometimes destroyed by war and invasion. Syria was invaded in 572 B.C. by Nebuchadnezzar, the King of the Babylonian empire. In the following years, Babylon itself fell to the Persians under Cyrus the Great who also took Syria. In 333 B.C. Alexander the Great conquered Syria as well as Egypt and Persia. For the next thousand years Syria was under the control of various rulers and empires.

The longest period of rule and stability was under the Romans. Pompey, Julius Caesar and Mark Antony all visited Syria at different times. The Romans presided over a developed society made up of many peoples and languages—Arabs, Jews, Phoenicians and Greeks, to name but a few. In general, life was settled and, compared to much of the known world, Syria was prosperous.

Under Roman rule, some local kingdoms flourished. The most astonishing was Palmyra. Located in an oasis on the edge of the desert, Palmyra was semi-independent of Roman authority. Under a succession of kings and queens, it grew quite powerful, especially in areas of trade. Eventually, under Queen Zenobia, it posed a threat to Roman rule. In the third century A.D. the Romans attacked and destroyed it. By that time, however, the city of Palmyra had grown in beauty and included many temples, theaters, statues and palaces. The miracle is that so much

**A close-up shot of one of the many ruined buildings of Palmyra.**

remains to this day. The ruins can still be seen, near the Syrian town of Tadmur. They are one of the most astonishing sights in the world.

Palmyra lies about 200 miles (320 kilometers) to the north of Damascus. After vast stretches of barren landscape, of windswept uplands with only scattered Bedouin and their flocks, Palmyra appears like a mirage on the edge of the desert. Coming upon it is like discovering a lost world. It is surrounded by the lush vegetation and palms of a huge oasis. Beyond it is the desert, empty and hot. The sheer scale of the ruined city is breathtaking. It is one of the most completely preserved ancient sites in the world.

The area immediately around Palmyra is full of relics. Tombs, palaces and castles, all from different periods of Syria's history, dot the landscape. Near the beautiful ruins of Palmyra there are tower-tombs—mini-skyscrapers used for the burial of important people and their families. An entire valley is full of these strange buildings. Not far from the city there is a Crusader castle perched high on a hill. Nearby is the dusty, modern village of Tadmur. There is also a small airport, and a luxury hotel stands amid the oasis palms. Within this one small area there are many elements of Syria's history: the glorious architecture of the ancient city with its Arab, Roman and Greek features, side by side with relics from the Middle Ages, and the airports and hotels which are part of the face of modern Syria.

Syria also played a role in the early days of Christianity. Damascus is mentioned in both the Old and New Testaments.

**The ruins of St. Simeon's Cathedral.**

Within a few years of Jesus' crucifixion, there was a Christian community in Syria. It was on the road to Damascus that Saint Paul experienced the revelation which made him become a Christian. The Bible also mentions the "street called straight" in Damascus; it was here that the early Syrian Christians lived and worshipped. The "street called straight" can still be seen today as it forms one of the main avenues in the old market, or *souk*, of Damascus.

One of the strangest of early Christian saints was Saint Simeon. He became a hermit and lived on top of a stone pillar for thirty years, preaching every day to the pilgrims who came to visit him from far and wide. The actual pillar and the monastery of Saint Simeon can still be seen in Syria today.

There are many Christians in modern Syria. The largest group

**The inner courtyard of the
Omayyad Mosque in
Damascus, one of the
holiest mosques in Islam.**

belong to the Eastern Orthodox church which has cathedrals,
convents, monasteries and places of worship in various parts of
Syria.

Despite being part of a Christian empire, ruled from
Constantinople (now Istanbul), Syria and its people never became
a Christian country. Islam, the religion which swept the country

44

and changed its history, came from deep in the deserts to the south, from Mecca in Arabia.

Islam exploded upon the known world in the seventh century A.D. after the death of the Prophet Muhammad. Arab armies stormed out of the Arabian peninsula and defeated all the armies and empires in their path. Syria was among the first conquests of the Muslim armies in about A.D. 635 and most of the people converted to the new religion immediately. Islam spread like wildfire, carried by victorious armies to Spain and Morocco in the west and as far as the borders with China in the east. With it came the Arabic language. Muslims believe that Arabic is not simply a language but the actual language of God. It also served to unite the many different peoples who now found themselves a part of the Islamic empire.

Because of its historical importance and its geographical position, Damascus became the first capital of the Islamic empire. The leaders of the empire were known as Caliphs. In Arabic, *Caliph* means "successor"—the Caliphs were the line of leaders chosen by the Muslim faithful to follow in the steps of Muhammad.

The Caliphs of Damascus belonged to a single family, the Umayyads. The Umayyad dynasty ruled the Islamic world for about one hundred years and their empire was even greater in size than the Roman Empire. In the years following A.D. 705, the beautiful Umayyad Mosque in Damascus was built. This is one of the holiest mosques in all Islam, after those of Mecca and Medina and the Dome of the Rock in Jerusalem. After about a hundred years, the power of the Umayyad Caliphs waned and the capital of Islam was transferred to Baghdad, in Iraq.

It was during that century, however, that the greatest Islamic expansion took place and that the Islamic way of life firmly took root. By then, Syria was Arab and Muslim in character and it remains so to this day. The emergence of Islam is undoubtedly the most important event in Syria's long and checkered history.

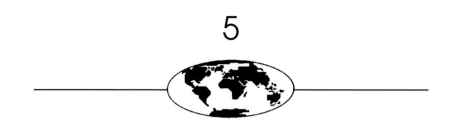

# The Islamic Way of Life in Syria

Six out of every seven Syrians are Muslims. Although there is a wide variety of other religious sects, mostly Christian, Syria is first and foremost a Muslim country. Islam is more than just the religion of Syria—it is a total way of life. In the cities, towns and villages, the mosques are the spiritual heart of the communities. From the tall minarets, the *muezzin* calls the faithful to prayer five times a day. Perhaps the most distinctive sound in all Syria is the cry of "God is most great," echoing from the minarets over the rooftops.

The Islamic religion began in Mecca, in Saudi Arabia. Muhammad, a merchant of the city, had heard God's voice in the barren hills and desert around Mecca. When he returned to the city and began preaching, telling the inhabitants to change their pagan ways, he was persecuted and had to flee to Medina. Soon, the number of his followers increased and then the people of western Arabia converted to Islam. In the century after Muhammad's death, the new religion spread rapidly.

**Syrian women crossing the courtyard of Damascus' Omayyad Mosque. Six out of every seven Syrians are Muslim.**

Islam, in Arabic, means "submission." For Muslims, Islam means submission to the will of God (Allah) and to the complete way of living set out in the Koran. The Koran is a complete record of the words of God, as spoken to Muhammad. Muslims accept it as the direct word of God. The Koran deals with every aspect of social, religious, political and economic life. One of its aims is that all mankind should be united in the Islamic religion.

Very early in the history of Islam there was conflict and division. After the death of Muhammad there was a dispute as to who should be his Caliph, or successor. One group believed the Caliph should be elected; another believed the title should be hereditary—that the Caliphs should be descendants of Muhammad and that the title should be passed on through the family line. As a result, Islam split into two main branches—Sunni Islam and Shia Islam. Shia Islam was further fragmented with arguments over the exact line of descendants.

The majority of Muslims throughout the world are Sunni Muslims. The strongest Shia community is Iran, though there are many Shia Muslims in Iraq and Lebanon. Syria's Muslims are overwhelmingly Sunni. There are, however, several other Muslim groups in Syria which are of interest—the Alawites, Druzes and Ismailis. Although these groups are small, they play an important part in modern Syria.

Syria has roughly half a million Alawites, mostly from the area around Lattakia, and over 150,000 Druzes in the mountain area of Jebel Druze. There are also Druze communities in the mountain zones of Lebanon and Israel. The religious origins of both these groups are obscure although they developed early on from branches of Shia Islam. One of the reasons that both communities have survived, often in the face of persecution, is that they have always lived in remote mountain areas away from the bulk of the population. This has given them the air of secret or closed communities. Even today, it is difficult to understand the nature of their religion and how it differs from mainstream Islam.

It is said, although it is not known for sure, that Alawites do not observe the holy Islamic month of Ramadan or make the pilgrimage to Mecca. Indeed, it is also said that they recognize some Christian feasts. Nevertheless, they are regarded in Syria as being part of the Muslim community despite their differences. The Syrian constitution specifies that the president must be a Muslim. In modern Syria, the Alawite community plays a major role in both political and public life.

The Druze religion is similarly obscure and believed to be very different from the Sunni Islam of the rest of Syria. The Druzes too are accepted as part of the Muslim community. Most of them still live in the harsh mountain terrain which has protected them over the centuries. They are a fiercely independent people with a reputation as good fighters and soldiers.

Another Muslim sect is the Ismailis. Their numbers are not so great and neither is their influence. There are Ismailis in many countries throughout the world, particularly in Asia. They acknowledge a living person, the Aga Khan, as their sacred leader. Again, despite obvious and serious differences, they are accepted as part of the overall Muslim community in Syria. One interesting historical fact about this sect is that, in previous centuries, it employed assassination as a weapon against its enemies. The killers bolstered their courage with the drug hashish and were called *hashashin*–hence the English word "assassin."

In Syria, therefore, religious differences are widely tolerated. It is Sunni Islam, nevertheless, which shapes the life and character of the vast majority of people. It is sometimes difficult for people of other religions elsewhere to understand the way Islam affects and influences every aspect of life for a Muslim.

The basis of Muslim belief is called the Five Pillars of Islam. The first Pillar is the *Shahada*, the profession of faith. To be a Muslim is to say and believe the following: "God is most great. I testify that there is no God but God and that Muhammad is His Prophet." The second Pillar is *Salat*, or prayer. All Muslims must face Mecca and pray five times a day. The prayers are said at dawn, midday, mid-afternoon, sunset and nightfall. They need not be said in the mosque. Muslims pray wherever they are—at home, in the street, in the fields or at work. Prayer is both a private and a public act. The third Pillar is *Zakat* and this involves giving charity and alms to the poor and needy.

The fourth Pillar is fasting. Every year, during the sacred month of Ramadan, Muslims abstain from eating, drinking and smoking during the hours of daylight. This can be very hard in a hot climate with long hours between dawn and dusk. Islam permits exceptions: travellers, the old and sick, and pregnant women are all exempt. During Ramadan, the period after dusk is a joyous one; everyone eats and drinks before resuming the fast at dawn the following morning. The end of Ramadan is signalled by the feast of Eid al Fitr. This too is a joyous time, with much celebration, family visiting and exchanging of gifts.

The final Pillar is the *Hajj*, the pilgrimage to Mecca in Saudi Arabia. For all Muslims throughout the Islamic world, Mecca is the focus of prayer. The Holy Mosque in Mecca is the most sacred place on earth. Once in a lifetime, each Muslim must try and make the pilgrimage to Mecca. The *Hajj* lasts about a week and takes place at a special time each year. Pilgrims from all over the world pour into Saudi Arabia and make their way to Mecca. Nowadays, the journey is relatively easy thanks to air travel. But it was not always so. In the past, going on pilgrimage involved a long and hazardous journey across mountains and deserts.

The pilgrim from Syria today rubs shoulders with a bewildering variety of nationalities at the *Hajj*. Muslim pilgrims converge upon Mecca from all points of the globe. Each pilgrim wears a simple white robe. There are no social distinctions and it is impossible to guess a pilgrim's background or status. Muslims believe that, before the eyes of God, all men are equal. The simple white robe is a symbol of this.

The religion of Islam shares many things with Christianity and Judaism. There are common prophets and traditions. Abraham, Isaac, Moses, John the Baptist and Jesus are all accepted by Muslims as part of their heritage. The crucial difference is that Muslims believe Muhammad to be the final Prophet and the Koran to be the final revelation of God.

Islam also differs in the degree to which it holds daily life and religion as inseparable. Social, legal, economic and spiritual matters are all covered by the Koran. If a Muslim wishes to find an answer to a problem concerning property, or divorce, or even how to prepare certain foods, he will find it in the Koran. One basic principle of the Koran is that people of all races, classes and colors are equal in the eyes of God.

One aspect of Islam is that there are no priests or clergy. There are people whose job it is to read the Koran and lead the faithful in prayer; there are also *muezzins* who give the call to prayer from the minarets and others who spend lifetimes studying and interpreting the finer points of the Koran. There are also people who interpret the Koran in terms of law and make decisions on legal issues which arise but are not necessarily covered in the Koran—this is particularly true in modern times.

Unlike the places of worship of other religions, inside the mosque there is no focus of worship like an altar. The inside of a mosque is usually a carpeted open space. The only real focus of attention is a small niche carved into the wall to indicate the direction of Mecca and therefore the direction of prayer. Outside the mosque there are

**A Syrian man washing before entering the mosque; cleanliness before God is a sign of humility.**

usually washing facilities; cleanliness before God is a sign of humility. Indeed, a Muslim in the desert or in barren mountains will often make the gesture of washing before praying.

The evidence of Islam is everywhere in Syria. From the grand mosques to the humble mud-built minarets on the banks of the Euphrates, Islam gives shape to Syrian life. It is the link between the city businessman in Damascus and the peasant in the fields, between the remote highland shepherd and the desert Bedouin.

Perhaps the real force of Islam is something greater still. To a Syrian Muslim, Islam offers a direct link with Muslims all over the world. The *Hajj* pilgrimage, with its enormous diversity of race, class and color, is the best expression of this. The differences between people of different backgrounds are overcome by the fact that they all share the same religious beliefs. Through Islam, Syria is not just a distinct country; it is part of a larger community of the faithful.

# 6

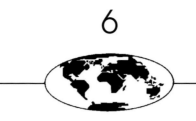

# The Crusades, the Mongols and Foreign Occupation

Syria was the site of the Crusades, the great battles between Christian Europe and the Muslim East in the eleventh, twelfth and thirteenth centuries. This was a turbulent time in the history of Syria and the wars gave rise to many stories and legends on both sides. In Europe it is often remembered as a period of heroic chivalry, of knights and kings fighting for Jerusalem and the Holy Land.

The European armies were led by the great and legendary figures of the day: Louis VII, King of France; The Holy Roman Emperor; Richard the Lionheart, King of England. On the Muslim side was the greatest of all the generals known to history–Salah al-Din, more commonly known in the West as Saladin.

The origins of these wars and campaigns were varied; the results were to have a major effect upon Syrian history to this day. Even now, all over Syria, there are gigantic castles and hilltop citadels left behind by the opposing armies. Some of the castles are in ruins

**The Krak des Chevaliers, the great Crusader castle.**

although others are still in excellent condition. The size and strength of these castles is proof of the vast scale of the Crusades themselves.

In the centuries before the Crusades, the capital of the Islamic empire had transferred from Damascus to Baghdad. Syria was merely an outlying province of the empire. It was invaded by people from Central Asia and Turkey called the Seljuks. The Seljuks were also Muslim and they established new states in Syria.

In Europe at this time, the so-called Dark Ages were drawing to a close. The period when most of Europe was uncivilized, disorganized, tribal and violent was over. New states had risen to power there—most notably the Normans, the Germans and the French, or Franks as they were then known. There was concern in Christian Europe that the Holy Lands and places around Jerusalem, in Palestine, Syria and Lebanon, were held in Muslim hands. To Europeans, this was the birthplace of Christianity. Jerusalem and Palestine were seen as part of the European and Christian heritage. The Pope called for a military expedition to be sent to the Holy Lands. Great armies of knights assembled in Europe. In 1096 the First Crusade began.

The Christian knights of Europe successfully invaded the Holy Lands, capturing much of what is now Lebanon, Syria and Israel. Jerusalem was taken in 1099. New states were set up, ruled by European princes and counts. The Christian armies were led by orders of knights, such as the Knights Templar. They took vows of poverty and obedience and fought under the sign of the cross. Despite early military successes, however, the knights never managed to capture any of the important Arab cities.

Gradually Muslim resistance grew in strength. The Arab armies found a great leader and general in Saladin, the ruler of Damascus. Saladin was respected by friend and foe alike and was renowned for his chivalry. In 1187 Saladin and his Muslim armies reconquered Jerusalem. In Europe, the news of the fall of Jerusalem caused great shock. The Third and final Crusade was launched to recover the Holy City. Among the leaders of the Christians was Richard the Lionheart, King of England.

The Christian armies failed and were matched in war by the

**A contemporary woodcut of the Christians fighting the Muslims. Despite hostilities, the Crusaders admired the Muslim leader, Saladin.**

Muslim armies under Saladin's leadership. The wars and battles continued for nearly another hundred years, punctuated by truces. Eventually, however, the European Crusaders were expelled. Syria, and the lands around it, became peaceful again. Saladin had been buried in Damascus as a great Arab hero.

The greatest of the castles still standing from this period is Krak des Chevaliers—the Fortress of the Knights. The castle is near the coastal mountain range, the Jebel Ansariya, and is one of the largest

58

and most dramatic castles in the world. The stronghold dominates the surrounding countryside. During the Crusades, the castle contained enough provisions and supplies to allow the defending knights to withstand a five-year siege if necessary. The Muslim armies failed many times to capture the Krak des Chevaliers and it was not until 1271, nearly two hundred years after the First Crusade, that it finally fell.

By this time the Crusades were almost over. They had been the first major conflict between the Christians of Europe and the Muslims of the Middle East. For the Christians it was a religious war and for the Muslims it was a war of liberation. The story of the Crusades is not just a story of battles: both sides developed

**Saladin, ruler of Damascus, the great Arab leader and general.**

a greater understanding and knowledge of each other. It was a meeting of different cultures. In centuries to come, Syria would again experience involvement with European powers.

Peaceful times, however, did not last long. In the fourteenth and early fifteenth centuries, Syria suffered great devastation and destruction. This time the invaders came from the East. Waves of Mongols under the leadership of Tamerlane invaded Syria and destroyed and plundered the cities. The Mongols were from Central Asia and their capital was the city of Samarkand. When they invaded Syria, castles, palaces and whole cities were reduced to ruins. Both Damascus and Aleppo were devastated by the ferocious attacks of the Mongols. Syria today is rich in antiquities but it would have been richer still had the Mongol attacks been repelled.

The Mongols left a trail of destruction in their wake: Syria suffered badly, with many of its population killed and its master craftsmen and artisans taken back to Samarkand as prisoners. In the years after the Mongol invasion, when Syria was weak, another power from the East stepped in and took control. The Turkish Ottoman Empire was to rule Syria for over four centuries, right up to 1918.

For much of this long period, Syria stagnated as a province of the huge Ottoman Empire. The Empire held sway over a massive area, covering southeast Europe, the Middle East and North Africa. The capital of the empire was Constantinople, now Istanbul. The Ottomans were renowned for their inefficiency. As a result Syria was an almost forgotten corner of

**A Turkish palace in Damascus, a reminder of the long period of Ottoman rule which slowly destroyed Syria's material and cultural wealth.**

the empire and was fragmented into small provinces. The country was not prosperous and became even poorer during the long, slow decline of the Ottoman Empire.

In the eighteenth and nineteenth centuries, however, another development was taking place which was to have a profound effect on Syria. The European powers, particularly Britain and France, began to take an interest in the lands under Ottoman control. They too had expanding empires and were seeking new territories. The French established rule in Lebanon (bordering on Syria) and the British took Egypt and control of the Suez Canal.

Gradually, the Ottoman Empire was dissolving and losing its power. For the people of Syria, after thousands of years of war,

61

occupation, division and invasion, the promise of independence and nationhood seemed a possibility. By the beginning of the twentieth century the Turkish Ottoman Empire was dying. The new powers in the area which Syria would have to deal with were European. Syria's modern history and its progress towards independence began at the time of the First World War (1914-1918).

# 7

# Modern Syria and the Path to Independence

In the years before 1914, the British and the French were major powers in the Middle East. For Britain, the Suez Canal was an essential lifeline to India and other parts of its empire. As the great powers of Europe prepared for war, they began to take measures to protect their interests in the Middle East. Syria was on the fringe of these momentous political events but it was, nevertheless, to play a vital part.

In 1914, Turkey entered the First World War on the side of Germany. Britain and France became her enemies. In the Middle East, the fate of the Ottoman Empire became tied to the outcome of the First World War. For all the Arab countries which had stagnated for centuries under Ottoman rule, the prospect of freedom and independence loomed on the horizon. And it was in British and French interests to foster rebellion against the Turks among Syrians and other subject Arab peoples.

The Arab Revolt of the First World War, as it came to be

known, marked the end of Ottoman rule in the Middle East. For the Arabs who fought in it, however, it brought mixed results. In 1914, Arab hopes of freedom were high. The British helped Sharif Hussein, the Governor of Mecca, to form a Bedouin army to attack the Turks. A key figure in the military campaigns was T.E. Lawrence, later known as Lawrence of Arabia. Turkish garrisons were attacked, railway lines were blown up and the Arab armies grew in confidence as the revolt itself grew. By 1918, British and Arab armies were advancing on Damascus. Liberation was in the air. With the Turkish collapse, most Arab nationalists believed the moment of independence had come. It was not to be.

The Syrians and other Arabs had been promised independence in exchange for their help in fighting the Turks. The British and French, however, had made a secret agreement in 1916. Their promise of independence to the Syrians was never meant to be kept. The secret agreement was that after the war, when the Ottoman Empire was broken and finished, Britain and France would divide the Arab lands among themselves and rule them. Some independence would be given to the peoples who inhabited the Arabian Peninsula. The Arabs of Syria, Egypt, Palestine, Lebanon and Iraq, however, would find that they were exchanging one form of colonial rule for another. Independence would be like a desert mirage.

In 1918, Damascus was finally liberated amid scenes of wild rejoicing. By the following year, however, at the Versailles Peace Conference, it was becoming obvious that Syria was not to have independence. The French controlled Lebanon and, under the terms of their secret 1916 agreement with the British, they took control of Syria in 1920. Their control was known as the French Mandate. Syria was divided yet again into several states and ruled by a French High Commissioner based in Beirut, the capital of Lebanon.

Most Syrians and Arabs felt a deep sense of betrayal. They had helped the British and French to defeat the Turks but had earned nothing. The French Mandate over Syria continued until the outbreak of the Second World War in 1939. It was a period of deep Syrian dissatisfaction. In 1925 a Syrian revolt was crushed by the French with great loss of life. There were some benefits under the French Mandate—many new roads and schools were built, a state system of education was developed and a university was built in Damascus. Overall, however, for most Syrians it was a time of frustration and unhappiness.

In 1941, after the fall of France, British soldiers occupied Syria. At the end of the Second World War, the British, French and Syrians negotiated the withdrawal of all foreign troops from Syrian soil. In 1946, Syria finally declared its independence. After thousands of years of turbulent history, of invasion and occupation, Syria was at last a free state.

Two years after Syrian independence, however, there occurred an event which most present-day Syrians would see as the greatest betrayal. In 1948, the state of Israel was established in the former lands of Palestine, directly next door to Syria.

Arabs everywhere believed that the Palestinian people had

been unjustly dispossessed of their homeland. Consequently they did not recognize the right of Israel to exist. Since 1948, Syria and Israel have been in conflict. This has led to wars on several occasions—in 1949, 1956, 1967 and 1973. It also led to severe problems for the new Syrian state.

The early years of independence in Syria were marked by instability. The government changed hands many times and there were several military coups, with the armed forces taking control. In 1958, Syria united with Egypt to form the United Arab Republic. There were several aims behind the union. It was thought that it would lead to the sharing of resources and increased development, especially in agriculture. Most importantly, however, some people believed it would be the first step towards the eventual union of all Arab countries.

In the 1950s, many Arab people had been stirred by the speeches of Egypt's leader, Colonel Nasser. Nasser was part of the new revolutionary movement which had taken power in Egypt from the old monarch, King Farouk. Nasser's political actions were dramatic and they excited Arab people throughout the Middle East. The Suez Canal was still owned and controlled by the British, but Nasser seized control of it for Egypt. Although this action led to a brief war with Britain, France and Israel in 1956, for many Arabs it was a key moment in their modern history. It seemed just and reasonable to break all links with the European powers and to regain total and independent control of their own countries and resources. There was much idealistic talk of unity in the Arab world and Nasser was a hero throughout the region.

The reality was different. The union between Syria and Egypt lasted only a few years and little was achieved. It was finally dissolved in 1961 when the Syrian military once again took control of the government from civilian leaders. Many of the officers who took part in the coup against the government belonged to a particular party or movement in Syria—the Baath Party. For a long period in recent Syrian history, the Baathists have been the dominant political force. In Arabic *baath* means "rebirth" or "resurrection." The Party's slogan is "Unity, Freedom, Socialism" and its main aim has been to create and

**Street signs in the bustling heart of central Damascus. On the left is a poster of Hafez al-Assad, who became president of Syria in 1971.**

develop state-controlled industry and agriculture as well as to promote its socialist politics.

Middle East politics are notoriously unstable, however, Hafez al-Assad's long stay in power (since 1971), has undoubtedly been a factor in the growing stability and development of Syria. This is particularly true in the light of the fact that there were over twenty changes of government in the first twenty-five years of Syrian independence.

Within Syria, the government has faced various problems. The population is increasing rapidly and many people are leaving the rural areas to move to the ever-expanding cities in search of work and a higher standard of living; this has led to housing shortages. The government is trying to reverse this drift, not least because Syria has superb agricultural potential. However, the main problems have arisen because of the various conflicts which have persisted since the end of the Second World War in this troubled region of the Middle East.

Syria has four times been involved, along with other Arab countries, in wars against Israel. The most devastating defeat was in 1967 when Israeli armies advanced to within 60 miles (95 kilometers) of Damascus. Syria also suffered greatly in the Arab-Israeli war of 1973. Power plants, ports and oil refineries were destroyed or damaged. Areas of southwestern Syria, notably the Golan Heights, were occupied by Israel. The cost of these wars has been enormous. As well as the economic damage, there has been great loss of life and human suffering. The wars have caused a huge influx of homeless refugees from the war zones.

Since the Lebanese civil war broke out in 1975, Syria has kept a large army on Lebanese soil. Initially, this was as a peacekeeping force. The civil war, however, became so complex, with so many different factions fighting each other, that Syria found itself getting more and more deeply involved.

For a time, Syria broke off political and diplomatic relations with Egypt, after Egypt entered into negotiations with the United States and Israel over the Palestinian problem. Similarly, with the outbreak of the Iran-Iraq war in 1980, Syria broke off relations with its neighbor, Iraq. This led to economic problems, since Iraqi oil was pumped to the Mediterranean ports via a pipeline which ran across Syria, and Syria gained substantial revenues from this. After earlier dreams of Arab unity, Syria now finds itself in an Arab world often divided by war and politics.

Throughout the Middle East, a major problem of recent years has been the growth of Islamic fundamentalism. Islamic fundamentalists want to return to a far stricter society with stronger Koranic law. They see all western influence as sinful. This is what has happened in Iran since the revolution and the rise to power of Ayatollah Khomeini; and many people in other Arab countries have hoped for a similar change. Modern-day Syria seems too liberal to many Islamic fundamentalists. Alcohol is on sale, even though it is forbidden in the Koran; and, while their counterparts in some other Arab countries follow Islamic tradition by wearing full-length dresses, with veils over their faces, and rarely go out in public, many Syrian women work outside the home and wear western dress.

**Syrian women at work on an experimental farm, transplanting seedlings. Unlike their counterparts in other Arab countries, many Syrian women work outside the home.**

In Syria, the fundamentalists are called the Muslim Brotherhood and are based mostly in and around the central city of Hama. There have been many attacks and assassination attempts on members of the government and ministers, as well as on the President himself. Violence has often broken out and the army has been involved in serious internal clashes with the Brotherhood. In particular, in 1982, there was major fighting in the Hama region. Islamic fundamentalism is seen by many other Arabs as a step backwards, a turning away from progress.

In Syria, as elsewhere in the Middle East, it continues to be a problem.

The problems faced by the Syrian government, then, are formidable. The short history since independence has been marred by coups, wars, regional conflict and internal problems.

In 1992, Assad was elected to a fourth seven-year term. During the Persian Gulf War, Syria joined the Allies in an anti-Iraq coalition. Assad looked to gain favorable attention from the United States for Syria's contributions to the war effort.

Peace talks between Syria and Israel have dragged on, as both sides are unwilling to make concessions on the issues of security, to agree on Israeli withdrawal from Golan Heights and to put an end to terrorist attacks on Israel from Lebanon.

Despite all this there has been considerable progress, both industrially and agriculturally. At the same time, in the midst of the seeming chaos, there has been growing stability.

# 8

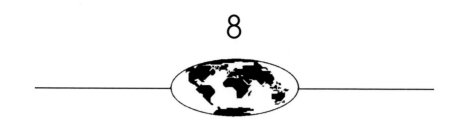

# The Economy

As befits a country that was part of the Fertile Crescent of ancient times, Syria is rich in agriculture. Unlike most Arab states in the Middle East, Syria is basically able to feed itself. An increase in agricultural production is nevertheless a key aim of recent planning. There is a similar aim to increase industrial development, and gradually move towards a more mixed economy, with industry and agriculture both playing a part.

The most impressive symbol of the modern change in Syria is the gigantic Euphrates Dam. The great hydroelectric turbines of this dam produce nearly all the electricity for Syrian industry and for the country as a whole. The great lake or reservoir created by the dam has led to a vast amount of newly irrigated land for cultivation. Both aspects of the Syrian economy, therefore, have benefited from this project.

Syria's economy is expanding in many new and different directions. This is largely as a result of several factors: economic planning aimed at creating a varied economy, huge energy

**Irrigation from the lake created by the building of the Euphrates Dam.**

resources (particularly electrical), an increase in the value of its exports, and loans and grants from other oil-rich Arab states. Syria also has oilfields of its own and has been able to export oil. All this has provided a sound base for expansion. Another factor is that the present generation in Syria is the first to be well-trained in the necessary industrial and technical skills; Syria's own manpower has become a major asset.

But this progress has not been easy. In the 1950s and early 1960s the industrial part of the economy was very limited and basic: there were few major roads, bridges, railways and ports. Irregular rainfall coupled with poor irrigation and old-fashioned farming methods meant that crop production was very bad. There were periods without rain, and Syria found itself having to import vast amounts of food. Many of the early industries were built up with the economic and technical aid of foreign countries—Italian, French, British, German and Russian—and had to be manned by foreign specialists because of the shortage of skilled Syrian manpower. Industrial and agricultural development was slow and costly. With the more stable political environment of recent years, however, much of this has changed. Planning has been sensible and practical and Syria has made great progress.

The main concern of Syrian industry in the 1960s was the processing of agricultural produce. Small factories produced canned fruit, juice, bread, cigarettes, cotton and olive oil. These industries are still important and, indeed, have grown considerably in size and efficiency, but the real areas of expansion are new. Like all modern nations, Syria has had to try and develop certain basic industries and raw materials. Cement, iron, steel, glass, paper and fertilizer are all essential not only to the growth of the country but also to the growth of other industries.

Most of the raw materials were readily available in Syria. After providing for its own requirements, the country is also able to export some of these commodities, thus gaining valuable revenue. In fact, Syria has huge resources of phosphates and it seems that in the near future, phosphates and fertilizer will become the country's main export.

There are cement plants in Aleppo and Tartous to supply all the country. This has been a prime necessity because of the

74

increase in construction. Enough cement is now produced for the domestic market, with some left over for export.

There are many other new areas of industry. Factories assemble a wide variety of goods—from television sets and electrical appliances to tractors.

One traditional industry which has grown considerably has been textiles. In ancient times, Damascus gave its name to high quality silk brocade—damask. Syria's reputation for textiles goes back thousands of years. Nowadays, cotton and cotton-polyester products are mass-produced in Syrian factories. This is a good example of how local and traditional handicrafts can be expanded into a major industry.

Syria also benefits from having its own oil resources. These are small in comparison to the huge oilfields possessed by some of its Arab neighbors such as Iraq and Saudi Arabia, but they are enough to satisfy Syrian needs. Until recently, the country has been able to export a large quantity of oil.

Syria's main exports, then, are cotton, textiles, phosphates, fertilizers and agricultural produce. There are plans to expand further into new areas. The Syrians hope to develop a plastics and chemicals industry using the natural resources of oil, gas and phosphates.

Fifty years ago, there was hardly any industry in Syria. Today it has a wide variety of heavy and light industries.

Another area which has seen spectacular growth is transport and communications. Syria stands at the crossroads of ancient and historic trade routes and yet, until recently, it possessed few modern major road and rail networks. Now there are new highways connecting not only the major towns and cities, but continuing into neighboring countries and linking up with international routes. The most dramatic expansion has been in the railway network. New lines have opened linking Lattakia with Aleppo and the northeast development areas, the port of Tartous with the central Syrian phosphate mines and Homs with Damascus. Hundreds of small roads have also been built, linking village to town and town to city.

Finally, there is one other industry which is growing rapidly—tourism. Syria is rich in attractions. There are not only the obvious attractions such as the ancient ruins but also Mediterranean beaches, coastal resorts and great scope for adventure tours in the mountains and deserts and along the Euphrates. Damascus and Aleppo and other key cities have a great deal to offer the tourists, not least their magnificent traditional *souks* (markets). At present, there is a program for building new hotels and holiday villas in certain areas and the government is investing heavily in tourist development. By air, western Europe is only a short journey—just a few hours—from Damascus.

To make that journey is to enter a different world of Arab markets, ruined civilizations, thousand-year-old mosques and ancient desert cities. Syria now realizes the enormous potential of tourism.

In the short span of Syrian independence, agricultural development has been less of a priority than industrial

**The oil refinery at Homs. Although Syria's oil reserves are small compared to those of some neighboring countries, they are sufficient for Syria's own needs.**

development. The population drift from the villages to the cities did not help this situation. Now the government is trying to change this and improve the agricultural performance. Over a thousand years ago, Syria was rich in wheat and other crops—it was the breadbasket of civilization. New plans to increase the area of cultivatable land may yet restore part of this image.

Lake Assad, named after President Assad, is a huge lake created by the dam on the Euphrates. The waters of this lake help to irrigate a huge area of land. This process has taken

77

several years to increase the production of a wide variety of crops. At present, the main crops are grains, sugar beet, cotton, tobacco and fruit and vegetables. The key grains are wheat, barley, millet and maize. Olives and pistachio nuts are also grown. Cotton was, until recently, Syria's principal export and there are plans to increase production.

The majority of the Syrian work force still work in agriculture. The number has been declining but, with all the new rural projects beginning, it should increase again.

Sheep, poultry and cattle are the leading livestock, and huge

**Weighing cotton. Until recently, cotton was Syria's principal export and there are plans to increase production.**

**An olive grove.**

new dairy farms are being established near the border with Jordan. Other animals raised include camels and goats. The goats are used for meat, milk and their hides, while the Syrian Bedouin are said to raise the finest camels in the Middle East. Finally, there are fish farms on Lake Assad. The most common species introduced so far is carp, with some growing as heavy as 220 pounds (100 kilograms).

The roots of Syria's history are based in agriculture. With all the new projects, the new irrigated land and the re-investment in rural areas, agriculture could be the basis of a prosperous future.

# 9

# Daily Life in Syria

In Syria today, just over half the population lives in cities and large towns. This is proof of the great changes which have taken place in Syrian society since independence in 1946. Many of these people are villagers, farmers and shepherds—newcomers to city life. Peasants still make up most of the rest of the population. In addition, there are still thousands of Bedouin roaming the huge Syrian desert and leading a life almost unchanged by the modern world. Many aspects of daily life are shared by all Syrians, although in some areas there are marked differences between city-dwellers, peasants and nomads.

It is in the *souks* (markets) that all the different elements of Syrian life come together. From the giant, sprawling covered *souks* of Damascus and Aleppo to small village *souks*, the social mixture that is Syria can be seen: the different lifestyles of the people—urban, rural and nomadic; the different races and languages—Arab, Kurd, Armenian, Turk; the different styles of clothing—modern, European, traditional and regional; and the

**A glimpse into the bustling *souk* of Damascus.**

different types of produce—agricultural, traditional handicrafts and international goods.

The *souks* themselves are like labyrinths, with winding alleyways, market stalls, tiny shops in old doorways and ancient mosques and shrines. It is easy for a visitor to get lost in the *souk*. Although the major cities have fashionable shopping centers and supermarkets as well, the majority of people still shop in the *souks*, especially in the smaller towns and villages.

Even in the cities, the *souks* are always crowded with what appears to be a chaotic throng. *Souks* are not only places to shop for spices, meat, vegetables or cloth, they are places to meet and talk, to haggle or bargain for the sake of it. Shopping centers and supermarkets may be more convenient but they are

81

essentially European or western. The *souks* are Arab. It is no accident that the *souks* are more than just trading or commercial centers; like the mosques, they are at the heart of all Arab communities.

In Syria, many traditional handicrafts still flourish. The products are sold in the *souks*: carpets woven from goat or camel hair, basket work and raffia, pottery, the heavy silver jewelry of the Bedouin often studded with large gemstones, embroidered cloth, copper and brass coffee pots and tables, engraved with intricate patterns known as arabesques and with passages from the Koran. The *souks* also sell one of the great handicrafts of Syria—wooden boxes, delicately inlaid with patterns of different woods. This craft (marquetry) is practiced throughout the country.

Some of these ancient and traditional handicrafts are dying out because of the rapid changes in Syrian life. Modern industrial methods can produce all these things in factories at greater speed and less cost. But many crafts still survive. Perhaps the fascination of the *souks*, especially in modern times, is to enter a world where old skills still exist and are openly practiced. Very often the craftsmen can be seen at work in their tiny shops, carving wood, engraving copper or weaving.

City life outside the *souks* is much as elsewhere in the world. The rhythm is dictated by school and work. From early in the morning the streets are busy with traffic and people. Outside the towns, life is obviously much slower as well as being poorer. Although farming methods are rapidly being modernized, many

**Clog-makers in Damascus *souk*.**

aspects of rural life are traditional. Life can be hard. People still have to rely on water drawn from wells and the ground can be difficult to cultivate. Many of the farms in Syria are run by state-controlled co-operatives—that is, the land and equipment are owned by the state and the people in the village work as a group.

The village communities are quiet by city standards. Often the houses seem very closed to the outside world. Traditionally, Arab houses are built around a central courtyard. In rural areas it is still common for large families to live all together—grandparents, parents and children forming a small community in themselves.

Repairing an irrigation pump. Many farming techniques in Syria are quite primitive, and improving irrigation to increase the amount of cultivatable land is one of the government's top priorities.

To the east and south, the Bedouin still live their hard and unchanging lives in the desert. Home is a tent and their life is one of constant movement. The Bedouin, with their flocks of sheep, goats and camels, are a link with an ancient past. For them, everything depends on rainfall and grass. Some years are good and some years are bad.

Perhaps the main difference between city life and rural life is obvious. Like anywhere else in the world, the cities are places of constant change, of strangers and new faces, of endless noise, of television and radio and the intrusion of the outside world. Village life has few of these things. People know each other and there is a strong sense of shared community. Often the people who arrive each year in the cities from the country try to recreate this feeling. An important factor in Syrian life, particularly for men, is going to the cafes for long sessions of tea- or coffee-drinking and pipe-smoking. The men play dominoes, cards and backgammon, and talk for long hours. It is not village life, but there is a community sense.

In the major cities, most men wear western clothes, such as a jacket, trousers and shirt. Many women also wear western fashions. Country people, and those who have recently arrived in the towns and cities, more usually wear traditional peasant clothes–baggy trousers, loose shirts and sandals. Some wear the traditional long, loose robes of the Bedouin, complete with the red and white checked headgear. Because of the rich diversity of people in Syria, there is an equal diversity of clothes. In the northeast, many women wear richly embroidered costumes, while elsewhere women wear long, black robes with a veil covering the head. This bewildering variety of clothes can be seen at its best in a busy place like the Damascus *souk*.

Syrian cuisine is similar to that of other Middle East countries: many dishes are based on roast or grilled lamb and chicken, usually accompanied by rice, chickpeas, yogurt and vegetables. There are, however, some distinctive foods. A popular lunch is *mezzeh*–a combination of many small dishes and savouries. Sometimes *mezzeh* is made of twenty or thirty different tiny courses; *hummous*–pureed chickpeas and ground sesame seed paste; pureed aubergine and lemon; meat rissoles; stuffed vine leaves; garlic and oil; crushed wheat; parsley, tomato and onion salad; olives; skewered kebabs of lamb; *falafel*—deep-fried balls of pureed chickpeas with herbs; pitta bread—the flat unleavened bread common to all Arab countries. The list of possible contents in *mezzeh* is endless.

There are many other interesting dishes, some introduced by the various conquerors and invaders throughout history. In Damascus, there are French restaurants dating from the period of the French Mandate. A wide range of home-grown fruit and vegetables are also eaten, including pistachio nuts from the Aleppo region, dates, figs, plums and watermelons.

One aspect of life in Syria that may seem dramatic is that all men must serve thirty months in the armed forces. Conscription is compulsory. Syria is always prepared for war and, considering

**A market scene. A wide range of locally produced fruit and vegetables is available in Syria.**

the history of this troubled region, this is hardly surprising. Soldiers are a common sight in most major towns.

Many Syrian women work–more women than in other Arab countries but the number is much less than in Europe. In rural areas, women have always worked in the fields and helped with the harvests. However, traditional feeling is still that a woman's place is in the home, looking after her husband and children. Nevertheless, women are playing a growing part in Syrian life. Thousands are graduating from the universities to become doctors, teachers and engineers. In many areas of local and provincial government there are now women in key positions. The rise in the status of women has been one of the most significant changes since Syrian independence.

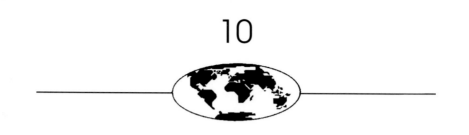

# 10

# The Cities and Towns

Although historically Syria has been primarily an agricultural country and part of the Fertile Crescent, the major cities have always dominated Syrian life. Damascus and Aleppo are thought to be among the oldest continuously inhabited places in the whole world. Damascus is even mentioned in the Book of Genesis in the Bible. In the quiet backstreets and alleyways of these great cities, it can seem as if little has changed in several thousand years. Indeed, within the cities there are ruins so ancient that a thousand-year-old mosque can seem like a recent addition. The cities reflect the long and varied history of Syria; they also project the newer face of twentieth-century progress.

Damascus, the capital, is Syria's largest city. Today the population is over six million. Damascus has boasted a settled population since the dawn of history. It has always been an important trade and political center. Long before it was the capital of Syria, it was the capital of Islam, a huge empire stretching from Spain to India. Before that, it was a key center of early Christianity

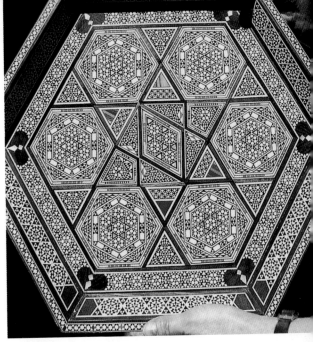

**A example of damascening, a craft which takes its name from the city of Damascus.**

and, before that, the capital of a Roman province. And long before that, it was the capital of local kingdoms which worshipped pagan gods.

Damascus has long been famous for its textiles and metalwork. As well as damask, in ancient times, the finest swords, weapons and other metalwork came from here. The iron or steel was inlaid with silver and gold in intricate patterns. The process is known as damascening, after the name of the city. Even the damson plum takes its name from Damascus: it was first grown in orchards outside the city walls.

The most important landmark is the Great Umayyad Mosque, dating from the early days of Islam. Even non-Muslims may visit this beautiful mosque (first taking off their shoes) and walk across

89

**A residential area on the outskirts of Damascus.**

the vast, internal spaces. The mosque is situated almost in the heart of the Damascus *souk*. The central courtyard is a peaceful haven from the thronged streets and noisy alleys of the *souk*. Much of this area has probably changed little over the last thousand years. The same time-honored handicrafts are on display—woven carpets and blankets, pottery, glassware and engraved copper. But Damascus is not just old and traditional.

Most of the city is modern and has been built during this century. There are wide avenues, modern office buildings and high-rise apartment blocks. There is a European atmosphere in some quarters with leafy streets, cafés, French restaurants and nightclubs. Today, Damascus is the political and administrative capital of modern Syria. The symbols of the country's progress are to be found here as well as the symbols of the past. Every year the Damascus International Trade Fair takes place. This is a huge trade fair involving over fifty countries and the latest scientific and technological exhibits. In a sense, history has turned full circle: once the crossroads of ancient trade routes, Damascus has now become the site of an annual international trade fair.

Aleppo is the second largest city in Syria and is situated in the north of the country. Its population is also around three million. Like Damascus, it is a city of great antiquity. Aleppo lies in a fertile bowl amid an almost tree-less barren landscape. Dominating the city is a huge rock upon which stands the Citadel of Aleppo. This was a fortified castle in ancient times. The present Arab castle dates from the Crusades of the twelfth

**The entrance to the Citadel of Aleppo, an impressive castle dating from the time of the Crusades.**

century and can be seen from far away. It is said to be the largest castle in the world.

Modern Aleppo is a commercial and industrial city. It is also the main marketplace for the agricultural regions of northeastern Syria and the Euphrates. Textiles and food-processing are the main industries. Again, like Damascus, Aleppo is a trading city. In a sense, its role has changed little since ancient times when it was the key destination and marketplace for the great silk caravans from the East. Even today, the covered *souk* of Aleppo is one of the biggest markets in the entire Middle East.

The two central cities of Syria are Homs and Hama. Both cities have populations of about a quarter of a million. They are both set in fertile countryside and most of their business is related to agriculture. Homs is also the site of oil-refining and phosphate industries. Hama is situated on the banks of the Orontes River

**A general view of Aleppo, Syria's second largest city.**

**One of the giant water-wheels of Hama.**

and is a major cotton-producing center. One of the sights of Hama is the giant water-wheels which were built in the fourteenth century to raise water from the river to irrigate nearby farmland.

Perhaps Syria's progress can be symbolized by the old waterwheels of Hama and the new dam on the Euphrates. Where the old wheels irrigate a few nearby fields, the new dam made over 2,500,000 acres (a million hectares) of new arable land.

The chief seaport of Syria is Lattakia, on the shores of the eastern Mediterranean. Lattakia's population is nearly a quarter of a million. It is a bustling port and the center of Syria's tobacco industry. It is also the leading holiday resort with good beaches, villas and tourist facilities. Other important towns in Syria include Tartous, the second major port, south of Lattakia. It is the chief export point for Syrian oil and phosphates.

Syria's cities are a mixture of ancient and modern. The country as a whole is covered with the ruins and remains of many early civilizations. In central Syria there is the magnificent ruined desert city of Palmyra. In the south of the country at Bosra there are extensive Roman ruins. Many of these ruins are the direct result of war.

Today there is a further testament to the ravages of war. In the southwest of the country, in the Golan Heights not far from the Israeli border, is the shattered ghost town of Quneitra. This was a town of over 40,000 people before the 1973 Arab-Israeli war. During the war it was captured by the Israeli army. The population was evacuated and the town was then totally destroyed by the Israelis before they withdrew. The Syrians have never rebuilt or repopulated Quneitra. Perhaps, in centuries to come, the ruins will be another part of Syria's heritage. In the meantime, it stands as a sad monument to the conflict in the Middle East.

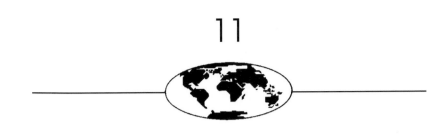

# 11

# Syria Today

After the troubled early years of independence, with military coups and constant changes of government, Syria seems to have found some stability. Recent years have been years of progress. Although Syria still has close links with Russia, it is completely independent. Indeed, much of the foreign money and aid which has helped Syrian development has come from western Europe as well as from extremely conservative Muslim states such as Saudi Arabia and Kuwait.

Syria is a socialist country but it has adapted socialist policies to its own needs. The banks and key major industries are owned and controlled by the state, as are the collective farms in the agricultural sector. Most land, however, is still privately owned and farmed. The economic system is flexible rather than rigid. Syria's main aim is to achieve prosperity based on a healthy and varied economy.

In a sense, the most serious problems facing Syria today and in the future come from outside the country. The key concerns are the conflict with Israel, the nature and purpose of Syrian military involvement in Lebanon, the problems of the Palestinian people, the effects of the Iran-Iraq war and Syria's own role in a divided Arab world. First, however, the internal problems have to be confronted.

Syria is a society made up of many different races and religions. While most live in harmony, some sections of the population are strongly opposed to the government. In particular, the Muslim Brotherhood, based around Hama in central Syria, are a constant problem. Their dissatisfaction with the present Syrian leaders has led to considerable unrest and violence. Similarly, although the nation is predominantly Muslim, belonging to the Sunni branch of Islam, many members of the government belong to the minority Alawite sect and this, too, has caused dissatisfaction. Elsewhere in Syria, groups like the Kurds in the north seek to establish an independent state for themselves. A prime concern in Syria, therefore, is to try and balance the interests of all these different groups. Any society composed of many races and religions must do this; if not there is a danger that it will fragment.

Another problem arises from Syria's desire to become an industrial country as well as an agricultural one. This is a healthy and practical aim, but again a balance must be struck. The population drift from country to city needs to be checked. If not, the plans for agricultural development will suffer. City life is a magnet for many rural Syrians, but life in the cities can be hard.

There are massive new housing developments but there is also a massive influx of people. Many come from the Syrian countryside but many are Palestinian and Lebanese refugees who have poured into Syria, and this has led to housing and job shortages. The pace of development in Syria is dramatic but so is the effect of wars and regional conflict.

If the country can resolve these problems, however, there should be few obstacles in the path of further progress. The changes in recent decades have been all the more remarkable in that they have often taken place despite all these difficulties.

Externally, the problems are more serious. The issue of Israel and the homeless Palestinian people is a major concern of all Arab countries. Egypt entered into peace negotiations with Israel, only to find itself isolated for a time from the rest of the Arab world. Although there has been considerable progress toward Middle East peace, Syria has thousands of Palestinian refugees in its territory and still sees itself as a front-line state in the Arab struggle against Israel.

Several wars with Israel have taken a heavy economic toll on Syria. At the same time, the need to be constantly alert and prepared for war has placed a severe strain on the Syrian economy. Syria maintains its army and air force in constant readiness, equipped with the latest Russian arms. The cost to the nation, in terms of manpower and money has been enormous. Despite recent advances, the Arab-Israeli conflict is a burden under which all Muslims and Jews in the Middle East still live.

Since 1976, Syria has maintained a large army in Lebanon. The role of the army has changed from being a peace-keeping force to being an active participant in the civil war. The Syrian army occupies part of Lebanon and can exert great influence over the future of the country. The reasons behind this costly occupation are varied—Syria certainly wishes to counteract Israeli influence in the south of Lebanon, but it also wishes to have a major say in who eventually controls the country. Like the Arab-Israeli conflict, this places a severe burden on the Syrian people and economy.

**Syrian soldiers. At the heart of a war-torn area, Syria maintains its army and airforce in constant readiness, at considerable cost to the nation in terms of both manpower and money.**

In addition, the war between Iran and Iraq and the Persian Gulf War increased tensions throughout the region. Syria, out of step with most of the rest of the Arab world during the Iran-Iraq conflict, gave its support to Iran instead of its eastern neighbor, Iraq. This led to further divisions in an already troubled and divided Arab world.

And yet, despite all these problems, Syria has made great progress. The last thirty years have seen some of the most dramatic changes in Syrian society for centuries. An industrial base has been created. Energy resources provide a sound foundation for further development. There are many new agricultural projects which promise a prosperous future. Even the tourist industry is expanding dramatically.

Syria has been the site of conflict and change for thousands of years: it is still the same today, except that the changes have meant progress and development.

# GLOSSARY

**Bedouin**    Nomadic tribes who live in the deserts of the Middle East.

**Caliph**    Leader of the Islamic empire.

**Fertile Crescent**    Ancient arc of land covering parts of what are now Syria, Turkey and Iraq. It was an area with very fertile ground, plentiful rain and large rivers conducive to farming; also called the "breadbasket of civilization."

*Hajj*    Pilgrimage to the holy city of Mecca.

**Five Pillars of Islam**    The rules of belief that the Muslim religion is based on. The five Pillars are: *Shahada, Salat, Zakat,* fasting, and *Hajj.*

**Islam**    Religion that follows the teachings of the prophet Muhammad.

**Koran**    Holy book of Islam similar to the Christian Bible.

**Mecca**    The holy city of the Islam religion, in Saudi Arabia.

**minaret**    Tower on mosques from which prayers are called.

**mosque**    Place of worship in Islam religion.

**muezzin**    Person in the Islamic religion who calls the people to prayer five times a day.

**Muslims**    Followers of the prophet Muhammad; members of the Islamic religion.

**souk**    Market.

**steppes**    High grassy plateaux.

**terebinth tree**    Tree that is the source of turpentine.

# INDEX

Istanbul, 44, 60

## J
Jebel Ansariya, 21, 58
Jebel Druze, 22, 31, 49
Jerusalem, 55, 57
John the Baptist, 52
Jordan, 7, 23, 79

## K
Khomeini, Ayatollah, 69
knights, Christian, 57
Krak des Chevaliers, 58, 59
Kurds, 10, 28, 32, 80, 96
Kuwait, 95

## L
Lattakia, 7, 20, 26, 31, 33, 34, 76,
    93-94
Lawrence, T. E. (Lawrence of
    Arabia), 15, 64
Lebanon, 7, 9, 11, 13, 19, 21, 49, 57,
    61, 64, 65, 71, 96, 97, 98
Lebanese Civil War, 11, 17, 69
Louis VII, King of France, 55

## M
Maalula, 16
Mari civilization, 39
Mark Anthony, 15
Mecca, 29, 45, 47, 49, 51, 53, 64
Medina, 47
Mediterranean Sea, 19, 20, 26, 28,
    69, 76, 93
Mesopotamia, 25
Mongols, 15, 16, 39, 60
Morocco, 30, 45

Moses, 52
mosques, 15, 37, 47, 51, 53-54, 89
Mount Hermon, 21
*muezzin*, 47, 52
Muhammad, 15, 29, 45, 47, 48, 52
Muslims, 9, 14, 32, 47-54, 97
Muslim Brotherhood, 70, 96
myrrh, 38

## N
Nabataeans, 39
Nabi Yunis, 21
Nasser, Colonel, 66
National Museum of Damascus, 40
Nebuchadnezzar, 15, 40
Normans, 57

## O
oil, 27, 73, 75, 94
Orontes River, 21, 93
Ottomans, 10, 60-62, 63, 64

## P
Palestine, Palestinians, 9, 57, 64, 65,
    96, 97
Palmyra, 14, 37, 41, 94
Persia, Persians, 11, 15, 16, 30, 36,
    39, 40
phosphates, 27, 74, 94
Pompey, 9, 15, 40
population, 7, 19, 33, 68, 88, 91

## Q
Quneitra, 94

## R
Ramadan, 49, 51